HUNTINGDONSI
Volume 3

A Portrait in Old Picture Postcards
of the towns and villages
in the northern half of the county

by
David Cozens

Foreword by
The Rt. Hon. John Major M.P.

S. B. Publications

By the same author: *Huntingdonshire Vols. 1 &2 — A Portrait in Old Picture Postcards*

First published in 1992 by S. B. Publications
c/o 19 Grove Road, Seaford, East Sussex, BN25 1TP

ISBN 1 85770 029 5

Printed by Geo. R. Reeve Ltd., Wymondham, Norfolk NR18 0BD.

CONTENTS

ACKNOWLEDGEMENTS

I have spoken with many people whilst checking the background to the various cards and I would like to acknowledge their help and encouragement. I am also grateful to those who have put up with inconvenient piles of paper, and those who have provided invaluable assistance in typing and proofing the copy.

I am especially grateful to those individuals and institutions who have given permission for the reproduction of this selection of postcards drawn from their collections.

From the collections of:-

Abbey Antiques, Ramsey	Nos. 6, 10, 11
County Record Office, Huntington	Nos. 36, 60—63, 67, 86, 93
Mrs J Edwards, Sawtry	Nos. 77—80, 82—83
Malcolm Fletcher, Huntingdon	No. 1
The Norris Museum & Library St. Ives	Nos. 12, 48, 51—53, 68, 71—72, 85, 89, 97—98, 101
Ted and Colin Pond, Bury	Nos. 5, 7, 14, 17, 23, 37, 39—41, 55—57, 59, 81, 84, 90, 99
Basil Spring, Godmanchester	No. 34
Mrs A Wills, Scotland	For the remaining fifty-four cards drawn from the collection of the late Don Wills

S. B. Publications publish a wide range of local history titles in the series "A Portrait in Old Picture Postcards". For details of current and forthcoming titles, write (enclosing S.A.E.) to:-

S. B. Publications, ℅ 19 Grove Road, Seaford, East Sussex, BN25 1TP.

FOREWORD

It is well known that my family and I have a great affection for the Old County of Huntingdonshire where we have lived for 15 years and which we regard as home.

Some years ago I agreed to become Patron of The Ramsey Heritage Trust, which will benefit from the author's royalties from this, the third volume of "Huntingdonshire in Old Picture Postcards". I understand that the Trust hopes to use these royalties to mount a permanent display illustrating the local and wider significance of the ancient Abbey at Ramsey.

May I express the Trust's gratitude to those who have made available these most interesting postcards.

As a relative 'new comer' it is fascinating to see these scenes from the recent past of my constituency.

The Rt. Hon. John Major M.P.

INTRODUCTION

As in Volume 2 the postcards have been arranged to suggest four excursions. The first is a circular tour based on Ramsey and to the east, the second on Huntingdon and to the west. The third journey commences at the Nene and continues through the Wolds to return along the A1. The final journey commences at Norman Cross and travels out into the Fens to return through the villages south of the River Nene. Once again some villages are not represented as I failed to find suitable cards and some in the north are less extensively illustrated since the appropriate cards have recently been included in other publications.

Ramsey the ancient ecclesiastical centre survived as a fen edge market town served by its docks and by two railway stations. Passing through Bury to Warboys, with its non-conformist tradition we journey on to Somersham then to Colne on the eastern limit of the 'County'. We return to Ramsey via the ring village of Woodhurst. In medieval times the greater part of this area owed allegiance to Ramsey Abbey, the exception being Somersham which came under the jurisdiction of Ely.

Leaving Huntingdon and Hartford, which were described in Volume 1, we move out of the Ouse Valley, pass RAF Wyton and take the minor but picturesque roads to Wistow and the Raveleys, turning at Little Raveley to Wennington, beware of the ducks! We arrive at Abbots Ripton, the home of two Peers of the Realm, follow the road alongside the railway then down Walton Hill and out onto the A1. Journeying south up Stangate Hill we pass over the flyover to Alconbury Weston and journey along roads north of the A14. This route includes the villages of Hamerton, Old Weston and Molesworth and so to Bythorn at the western limit of the 'County'. We return via a diversion to Keyston, cross the A14 and pass through Leighton Bromswold and Woolley down a minor road to Alconbury and back to Huntingdon via the Stukeleys.

The northern limit of Huntingdonshire lies halfway across the bridge over the River Nene between Sibson cum Stibbington and Wansford, from here we travel via Elton, south down the Bullock Road to Glatton swinging out through the Giddings to Sawtry. We return along the Great North Road through Stilton and Water Newton.

Our final journey starts at Norman Cross continues into the Fens via Conington and Holme through Ramsey St Mary's and Ramsey Heights to Upwood. Through Ramsey and alongside Bodsey House to Ramsey Mereside we reach the fen edge settlements of Farcet and Stanground. Travelling south of the Nene through the Ortons and Alwalton we regain the A1 and travel south to return to Norman Cross.

Many of the cards show street scenes photographed or published by local individuals. A fair number of the cards show views and Inns along Ermine Street, the York Road and the Great North Road from a time when it was not necessary to divide the carriageway into southern and northern lanes, let alone provide dual or multiple carriageways. It is difficult to appreciate that the roads shown on Vinegar Hill, through Little Stukeley or through Water Newton were sufficient for the traffic of the day. Two of the Great Northern Railway Stations shown have been demolished in the interests of speed and efficiency and two others on subsidiary lines, together with their tracks, have also been removed. In this volume we shall see a hospital used as a church, a country house as a hospital and airfield buildings as a sanatorium. During these journeys we shall encounter famous "Huntingdonshire families" such as the Cromwells, the Probys, the Cottons, the Ferrars, the Gordons and the Fellowes. At various locations we shall meet school groups and people, in bands, at reunion meetings, working on the land or attending an outdoor baptism. We shall meet a famous cockerel, a pets' cemetery and the inevitable ghost.

This northern section of the 'County' contains several domestic houses of significance as well as interesting churches with their monuments, fittings and furniture. Elton Hall and Ramsey Abbey may be visited as can most of the churches.

For those born in Huntingdonshire and who have lived to see many changes I trust these cards will have revived pleasant memories. I hope that this series of three small volumes will encourage 'the new comers' to venture out and discover the contrasting scenery and history that lies within the boundaries of Huntingdonshire.

David D Cozens,
Bury,
November 1992.

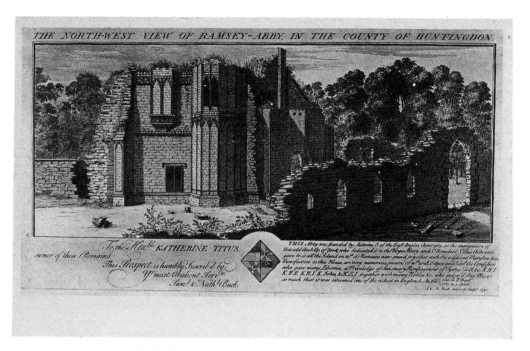

RAMSEY, THE ABBEY GATEHOUSE

This card by Wood of Huntingdon reproduces the Buck Lithograph of 1730 showing the remains of the 15th century Gatehouse to the Abbey. A large section of the Gatehouse was taken to Huntingdon by the Cromwell family in the 16th century to provide an entrance to Hinchingbrooke. The present day structure at Ramsey incorporates a 19th century extension across the driveway leading to the house created in the grounds. Established in 969 AD the Abbey was for nearly 600 years a very influential and wealthy institution. At its dissolution in 1539 the Abbey at Ramsey was judged to be worth more than the Abbeys at Peterborough or Ely or Lincoln.

RAMSEY ABBEY, SOUTH ASPECT

The Cromwell family used part of the Abbey as a dwelling. This card, posted in 1911, shows the 13th century buttresses of the underlying ecclesiastical structure. The central square bay windows, probably also the porch further to the west, are from the 17th century. The west wing was added in the early 19th century and somewhat later the whole of the top storey and on the eastern face the projecting windows and the staircase. The function of the original ecclesiastical building has not been established. In 1737 the Abbey was acquired by the Fellowes family who became Lords De Ramsey in 1887. In 1937 the House was leased to the Grammar School.

CHURCH, RAMSEY, HUNTS.

52687 ⒲

RAMSEY, CHURCH OF ST THOMAS OF CANTERBURY

The most substantial survival of the ancient abbey is it's hospital. The arcades and the chancel date from the late 12th century. Early in the following century the hospital building was consecrated as the parish church of Ramsey. The external walls of the aisles were erected in the 15th century and the tower in the 17th. As can be seen therefore this is a most interesting church. In passing it may be noted that in Huntingdon part of the somewhat similar hospital of St. John now houses the Cromwell Museum.

RAMSEY, HIGH STREET

Posted in 1905 this card looks westward along the High Street. On the left-hand is the old post office building prior to the addition of the upper storey. The gabled roof showing further along belonged to the 17th century Rose and Crown Inn, now demolished. Happily the adjacent properties remain, if somewhat altered. Across the street the buildings have survived virtually as shown; from the implement shop, currently Fenland Hardware, down to The Angel. Reflecting quieter days Bill Miller the carrier waits for his custom and a cat walks down the road.

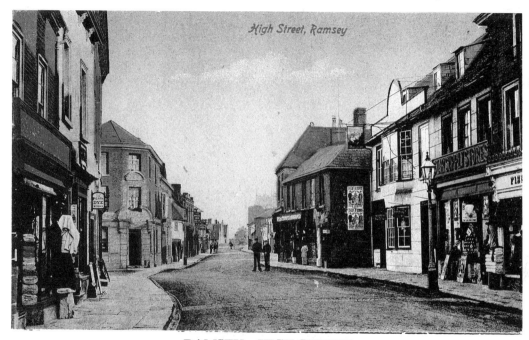

RAMSEY, HIGH STREET

This Freeman card looks eastward towards the church. It is interesting to note the raised pavement crossing the Great Whyte junction on the left. On the right Sheif's shop, projects beyond the George Hotel. In medieval times the Great or High Bridge crossed the Bury Brook at this point. Today the shop has been replaced by the National Westminster Bank set in line with the hotel frontage; the Brook still flows beneath the bank and the road.

RAMSEY, TOWN BAND

Photographed at the harness maker's workshop in the George Yard this card shows the drummer, Mr Whitwell, the base player, Mr Goats and next Mr Greenwood.   The money collector was Mr Noble and the other drummer was Snapper Hutchcraft.   The other four players were not identified on the card.

GREAT WHYTE. RAMSEY. (HUNTS.)

RAMSEY, GREAT WHYTE

At one time the Bury Brook ran along the length of the Great Whyte in an open water course; this was enclosed in 1852. The memorial clock was erected in 1888 to honour the 1st Baron of Ramsey, the Rt. Hon. Edward Fellowes; it was restored in 1988. Since this photograph was taken the railings around the memorial have been removed as has the thatched cottage at the junction of New Street. The roof of the shop that was until recently Davidson's has been raised. The wall in front of The Grand has been removed and the windows and dormers of the adjacent cottage have been remodelled. The charabanc on the left may well be one of those once operated by Ernie Pond.

RAMSEY, THE DOCKS

The mill erected in 1892 by T.F. (Tom Flowers) was converted by D.S. (David Sutton) in 1983 to become the River Mill Apartments. These were formally opened in 1984 by the Member of Parliament for Huntingdon, John Major. The conversion has retained the loading bay doors on the first floor. This card by J. Freeman of Ramsey, posted in 1919, shows sacks being lifted on or off a wagon. This photograph was taken at the time of the 1912 floods. The docks have been modified to receive pleasure craft. None of the buildings to the right remain.

RAMSEY, HIGH LODE

Bury Brook flows into the High Lode at the docks; the Lode joins the Old Nene River approximately 1 mile further along.   The High Lode industrial development now lies to the right. The house, walnut tree and cottage are no more. In the distance to the left can be seen the old fertiliser factory. This card, posted in 1910, shows the barge floating well below the top of the bank. (See previous page.)

FUNERAL OF LORD DE RAMSEY

At midday on the 14th of May 1925 a special train from London drew into Ramsey North Railway Station. The coffin was carried along the platform and placed onto a wagon lined with laurel leaves. Drawn by two horses the body was carried to the Parish Church for the funeral service and internment.

RAMSEY NORTH RAILWAY STATION

A happier gathering, we seem to be looking at a wedding party from the 1st World War period. I wonder who they were?

High Street, West Ramsey

RAMSEY, HIGH STREET WEST

Post marked 1911, this card looks along the one time Bridge Street. The Eagle Chambers, with advertisements for postcards in the window of Palmer's shop, have been replaced with the offices of the Nationwide Building Society. The eagle has been relocated around the corner and continues to look down at the passing traffic. The eagle originally surmounted a Columbian printing press; it signified the American nationality of it's inventor. The press is now in the Museum of Technology in Cambridge.

High St., Ramsey, Hunts.

RAMSEY, HIGH STREET

One of the series of the S.P.T. & P.P.C. Co. of Glasgow! This card was sent from Ramsey in 1905. One of the advertisements seems to be a recommendation to 'fry your fish and pancakes in Atora English Beef Suet'.

1106. High Street, Ramsey.

RAMSEY, HIGH STREET

The range of cottages on the corner of School Lane have been replaced by the Temperance Court. Beyond rises the spire of the 1899 Methodist church. In 1942 the main church building suffered bomb damage, as a consequence two marriages took place in the school room. One couple were Mr & Mrs Bebe. Who were the other couple? Further along is the shop once used by George Proud and Sons for their bicycle business. The premises now accommodate the Copping's hairdressing saloon. The railings on the right stand in front of The Gables, a house with long standing medical connections and one which retains structures from the 14th century.

RAMSEY, BIGGIN MALTING

In the 14th century Biggin grange supplied the Abbey with milk, butter and cheese. From the records it seems that by the 15th century it was a scene of relaxed discipline causing the Bishop, to take the community to task! The Cromwell family lived at Biggin but in the 18th century the property ceased to be residential. The card, posted in 1906, appears to show a partially thatched ruin. The building was approached from Biggin Lane and was eventually demolished in the Second World War in connection with the development of R.A.F. Upwood.

Bury Village, Hunts

BURY

Since the majority of this view lies this side of Bury Brook perhaps we should be referring to Hepmangrove! The thatched dwelling and the Post Office next door are no more, we are looking at an area between todays Bury Stores and R Housden's building yard. To the left the cottages are presumably the Old Forge beyond which can be seen the Old School.

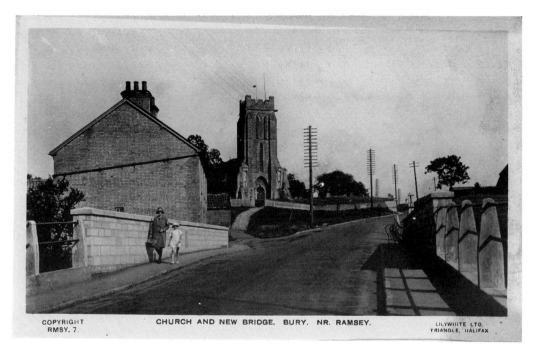

CHURCH AND NEW BRIDGE. BURY. NR. RAMSEY.

BURY, CHURCH AND NEW BRIDGE

Upon the hill can be seen the 13th century tower of Holy Cross, which once served an area that included Ramsey before the town gained it's own church dedicated to St. Thomas of Canterbury. The tower was added to an earlier structure. The masonry against the western face of the tower is somewhat of a mystery, there may have been a chapel in this position. The line of the footpath to the church has changed since this photograph was taken.

BURY, THE BROOK

The fields shown on this card are now incorporated into the Ramsey Golf Course. The cottage to the right, once the home of the Pond family, has been demolished.

WARBOYS, RAMSEY ROAD

Published by Gabbitas of Warboys this card was posted in 1918. At the time the photograph was taken residential development stopped at the white gate which led into a large field. Since then the house, this side of The Laurels on the right, has been demolished and the high wall considerably lowered, although the original height may still be indicated on the boundary between Nos 29 & 30 Ramsey Road.

HIGH STREET — WARBOYS

WARBOYS, HIGH STREET

Printed in Berlin and published by Gabbitas this shows the view looking eastward along the High Street. Just in the picture on the right is No 10 and beyond, end on to the road, No 12. Somewhere in the region of No 16 can be seen the sign of The Lion. In the middle distance on the left is No 21, until recently occupied by Godfrey's the Butchers. The bell of the old school is just visible above the roof. It is interesting to note the lack of pavements. The non segregation of vehicle and pedestrians imparts a sense of community lessened in these days of 'through traffic'.

WARBOYS, HIGH STREET

Another Gabbitas card this would appear to show the Sunday School pupils of The Grace
Baptist church just in view on the right. Forge Way now joins the High Street over to the
left behind the children.

Mill Green, Warboys.

WARBOYS, MILL GREEN

Published by J.S. Gabbitas this shows the windmill across the Weir. Modern buildings now close the view beyond the water. The Victorian lamp standard is still present in front of the Weir, although the lamps have been replaced. The view to the left is much as shown but with the removal of some of the boundary walls.

Public Baptism at Warboys.

WARBOYS, PUBLIC BAPTISM

In the newspaper cuttings held by the Norris Museum and Library in St Ives there is an account of the baptism of twelve people by total immersion in the Weir. Apparently 3,000 Particular Baptists gathered on the eighth of April 1905 to observe the service conducted by Pastor Marsh. Card published by Gabbitas.

HEATH ROAD, WARBOYS

WARBOYS, HEATH ROAD

From the height of some 65 feet above sea level this situation affords a panoramic view across the Fens towards Chatteris. Today's A.141 crosses the Fen along the same route but as it approaches Warboys it turns right at the dwelling behind the trees and climbs up to the roundabout. This card, posted in 1922, was published by B Harvey of the Warboys Post Office.

WARBOYS
MR FYSON WITH HIS
V.C. COCKEREL

Frank Fyson J.P. eventually raised £25,000 for the wounded soldiers of the First World War. In 1919 the bird was finally auctioned for £100. The purchaser, Mr G.A. Wotten, was apparently going to preserve the cockerel. Does this mean that this famous fowl is still in existence somewhere?

Somersham. *Rectory Lane*

Valentines Series 49292

SOMERSHAM, RECTORY LANE

Since this photograph was taken the row of cottages on the right have all but disappeared. Much of the ground level frontage remains but with infilling of the doors and windows. For an insight into the local history of Somersham talk to the man behind the wall, Mr Grimwood! The left hand side of the lane has been redeveloped; the card was posted in 1913.

Squire's Lane, Somersham

Valentines Series   49293

SOMERSHAM, SQUIRE'S LANE

Posted in 1908 this card depicts Manor Hall before the upper storey was removed. The building was erected in 1720 by Squire Thompson around an earlier structure, the chimney-stack dates from the 16th century. The ground floor windows each side of the central arched entrance are now doorways to Nos 21 and 23 Parkhall Road, which is the current name for Squire's Lane. Today Grange Road joins Parkhall Road this side of the Manor House. The trees in front of the House have been felled.

Somersham. *Church Street*

Valentines Series 49294

SOMERSHAM, CHURCH STREET

Church Street gave access to the parish church and to the Bishop of Ely's Palace. The Palace, dating from the 12th century, was selected to be Catherine of Aragon's prison but was eventually rejected in favour of that of the Bishop of Lincoln at Buckden. The card, posted in 1909, shows the fire engine station, since demolished and the school. A stone records that the school was founded by Thomas Hammond Esq. in 1747 aided by a grant of land from the commoners 1747, erected 1782. It reminds the pupils "Improve your time so make amends for this donation of your friends".

SOMERSHAM, HIGH STREET

Taken alongside the shop at No 27 this photograph shows The Brewers Arms, now The Fairway. Across the road, just in view, is No 20; it is currently being carefully restored. The porch beyond the figure standing in the street appears to have been subsequently raised to the level of the roof of the main building.

No. J. & S. 7286

STATION ROAD, SOMERSHAM.

SOMERSHAM, STATION ROAD

This card was sent with birthday greetings in 1912; it was one of the Webb's Series, Somersham. Today Brockfield has lost the rear left chimney but has gained large bay windows and a new porch. The white fence is also no longer with us, just to the right of the far brick pillar there now stands a replica of the pump erected by the Feoffees in 1870.

SOMERSHAM, STATION

"Have sent you a view of our station, Dad is on there if you can pick him out". To help, the sender has placed crosses above and below the second gentleman from the right. This card was posted in 1906. The lines from Chatteris and from Ramsey East met beyond the station.

COLNE

Taken alongside the Baptist Chapel, now Chapel Cottage, the photograph looks towards a 16th century building with a large central chimney bearing three octagonal shafts. The building provides two dwellings, Dovecote and Dove Cottage. In the foreground are Langley House and The Poplars on the right and left respectively.

WOODHURST, CHURCH STREET

This card was posted in 1910 as a Christmas Card. Church Street with the parallel South Street and the short linking roads at each end make Woodhurst a fine example of a ring village. On the left is Old Farm, the adjacent two small cottages have been demolished since this photograph was taken. Beyond stands Erin House, without it's Tiger Moth embellishments! and next the Post Office. The houses seen in front of the church of St John the Baptist have been replaced.

Wyton Hostel Huntingdon.

WYTON, AIRFIELD

Climbing up from the Ouse valley to the left can be seen R.A.F. Wyton. Opened in 1916 Wyton's role was to train airmen prior to active service, to provide among other things at least 15 hours solo flying! Just prior to closure, in 1919, the station hosted men of the American Flying Corps. In 1919 some of the buildings were used, as shown in this card, as a sanatorium or hostel where youngsters could benefit from the country air. By 1935 the site was being redeveloped once again as an airfield.

Church Street, Wistow, Hunts. Dear & many thanks for Book - will call & see you before the

WISTOW, CHURCH STREET

Published by J. Freeman & Son of Ramsey this card was posted from Bedford in 1906. To the left can be seen The Plough and across Bridge Street the village post office. The post office and the adjacent cottage are now one dwelling, The Shieling; The Plough is also a private residence.

WENNINGTON

This jug was found beneath the hearth of a cottage during demolition in 1914. Probably made in the 17th century the design mocks Cardinal Bellarmine. The burial of this jug containing a lump of clay stuck with pins was probably intended to combat witchcraft.

ABBOTS RIPTON, THE HALL

Lord De Ramsey and his family took possession of the Hall in the 1930's. During the 1st World War the Hall, as all houses of suitable size, was pressed into service as a hospital to take care of the returning casualties. This photograph, taken by Slater of Sawtry at Christmas time, shows some of the patients and nurses.

ABBOTS RIPTON, THE MOAT HOUSE

The second Peer of the Realm to reside in this small village is the Lord Renton, who prior to his elevation, served the Huntingdon constituency in the Lower House for 34 years. Part of the De Ramsey Estate, this house partially surrounded by a moat, is a timber framed building dating from the 16th century. The origin of the médieval gargoyle between the two upper windows is not known.

ABBOTS RIPTON, RAILWAY STATION

Looking down the Great Northern line with the aqueduct and the road bridge to Wennington in the distance. Not far from this spot in the winter of 1876 a multiple collision occurred when frozen signals could not be moved to stop oncoming traffic. Since the accident a fail-safe procedure has been adopted whereby signals are set to "stop" and require action to change them into the "go" position. Inter City passengers speed by probably unaware that this station ever existed. This card was posted in 1920.

SAWTRY, A1

Major re-surfacing about to be implemented by employees of the Whitehall Asphalt and Engineering Company Ltd., near the junction of the A1 with the B1090. Civil engineering on a somewhat different scale to that currently underway further south on the A1! Incidently in Volume 2 the A1 at Buckden was incorrectly identified as Mill Road.

THE WHEAT SHEAF INN. ALCONBURY HILL. 2.

ALCONBURY HILL, THE WHEATSHEAF

This Direction Stone stands close to the junction of Ermine Street and the Great North Road with London 72 miles away via Cambridge, 64 miles distant through Royston or 68 through Biggleswade! The Bullock Road also came in nearby from the North West. An appropriate position therefore for a coaching inn. The Wheatsheaf in it's day was considerably larger than the Inn depicted above. The Crossways Distribution Centre now occupies the site. The cottage on the right has survived; but not the ball filial on the stone, it had to be replaced following an accident.

THE HILL, ALCONBURY WESTON.

ALCONBURY WESTON, THE HILL

The York Road, climbs up Vinegar Hill to meet the road from Huntingdon and Royston. The current A.1 which bypasses the Alconburys to the east has been expanded to a dual carriageway and is about to consume even more land as it is further upgraded. The telegraph posts march along this arterial route and will appear in other cards! The built-up area has expanded beyond the White Hart with the development of Tangle Wood, in between lies Apple Tree House. Across the road the village shop remains, alongside it has been built Poplar House. Beyond, just in view, is Old Forge Cottage.

THORNS GATEWAY.

ALCONBURY WESTON

ALCONBURY WESTON, THORNS GATEWAY

A picturesque view looking across to the road leading to Hamerton. The large tree has gone but some of the fencing remains. The thatched roof has been tiled. The Limes to the right has lost it's chimneys since this photograph was taken.

HAMERTON

Today brambles grow across the door and under the window behind the pump: the pump itself no longer stands by the roadside. Otherwise the building remains much as shown. Fate has been less kind to the cottages further along, they have disappeared. Did the folk gathered together live in the cottages or were they visiting the Parish Room which lies up the lane?

OLD WESTON VILLAGE

OLD WESTON

Continuing through Winwick we arrive at Old Weston. This card by Goggs of Huntingdon looks back up the hill. The view from Brook Farm House shows in the distance Fairmead before it was enlarged. The shop on the left has been demolished. The window and door of the house with the slate roof have both been bricked in since this photograph was taken. Set in the wall of the white building with the three dormers is a stone plaque dated 1622. A new dwelling has been built alongside. The main road was realigned to serve Molesworth airfield leaving St. Swithin's church seemingly detached from the village.

Dogs' Cemetery, Molesworth, Huntingdon.

MOLESWORTH, PETS' CEMETERY

In the early part of this century Molesworth was the last resting place of many faithful companions. The pets remembered were not just dogs as the card implies. In more recent times 'Molesworth' has been synonymous with the Cruise Missile, deployed to protect our Western values. Thankfully this is no longer considered necessary.

Bythorn

The OBELISK.

BYTHORN, THE OBELISK

Posted in 1906 this card shows "Mrs Griffith's house". T Brown and Son's Obelisk Farm still exists south of the A14 right on the westernmost boundary of the county. The building itself has been modified, the right hand wing has been enclosed with the loss of the verandah and the shutters have been removed from the other wing.

KEYSTON, THE WHITE HORSE

Since this photograph was taken The White Horse has undergone a transformation to become The Pheasant. The sapling on the green has grown into a mature tree. At Keyston we are just within the county, to make this clear to all, one of the County signs is prominently fixed to the building. The Pheasant has been provided with a new thatched porch and a new door has been inserted beneath the right hand dormer.

KEYSTON, HILL FARM VIEW

Returning to the A1/M1 link road from The Pheasant the view today remains almost as shown. The garden wall beyond The Stone House has been modified and the thatched cottage has been partially demolished. Hill Farm stands on the rise in the distance.

LEIGHTON BROMSWOLD

The thatched building to the left is no longer with us, however The Forge Cottage and The Forge still remain. The lychgate erected in memory of church warden George Smith is notable by it's absence. The photograph must therefore have been taken before 1909. The stone denoting the meeting place of the Hundred now rests by the lychgate. The tower of the church of St. Mary was erected by the Duke of Lennox in 1634. Some eight years earlier George Herbert had started the refurbishment of the interior, the resultant 17th century fittings are well worth a visit.

LEIGHTON BROMSWOLD, GATEHOUSE

Originally built in the 17th century as a gatehouse to a much larger structure. It has not been established if Sir Gervase Clifton completed his mansion. The central carriageway was enclosed and the premises became the Vicarage. This photograph was taken before the 1904 alterations. The present occupant of the house, the Reverend Robert Van de Weyer is chairman of the Cambridgeshire Historic Churches Trust.

Salen. Wood. Leighton.

LEIGHTON BROMSWOLD, SALEN WOOD

Yet another Christmas posting! The site of Salen Chapel was excavated by Dr. Garrood just south of Salome Wood. The figure in the car is Janet his wife. In Norton's map of 1680 the wood is called Sallam Wood. This card was sent to Sidney Inskip Ladds in 1927.

WOOLLEY,
ST. MARY'S CHURCH

This card was published by Ernest Whitney from his Electric Studio in Huntingdon. The tower and spire were restored in 1932. What was essentially a 13th century church with a 14th century tower was in ruins by the mid 1950's. The Russian Prince Mikepher Alphrey was a rector of Woolley and was reappointed to his former position at the Restoration.

BOTTOM BRIDGE ALCONBURY

ALCONBURY, BOTTOM BRIDGE

One of the Goggs Art Series this card shows the old wooden footbridge. Brook House and The Old Red Brick House can be seen to the right of the figure. New buildings have taken the place of the white house shown further to the right. The Alconbury Brook rises in Northamptonshire just over the county boundary and joins the Great Ouse alongside Huntingdon castle.

ALCONBURY, CHAPEL STREET

A Maddison and Hinde card showing in the background the 16th century Manor House, now a restaurant, and in the foreground on the right the barge boards of the barn alongside today's No. 4 Chapel Street. The properties between the Methodist Chapel and the Manor House have been replaced. On the left No. 13 is little changed. No. 14 is now one dwelling, rather than the two depicted; beyond can be seen the bay window of No. 19. At sometime the chimneys have been removed from number 27.

LITTLE STUKELEY, THE SWAN AND SALMON

Standing alongside Ermine Street is the old Swan and Salmon Inn. The panel on the chimney stack shows a chained swan with the initials C and E D for Christopher and Elizabeth Druell with the date 1676 and below a salmon. The gradients through Little Stukeley have been eased and the present road surface has been raised to the level of the first floor. The Swan and Salmon is now a private residence. The Forge Cottage remains on the other side of the minor road.

LITTLE STUKELEY, ERMINE STREET

It is of course no longer possible to take the indicated road to Abbots Ripton. The runways of RAF Alconbury have closed the old route. Since this photograph was taken the dwellings on the left have been demolished. Post Cottage on the corner of Church Way has been extended towards the Union Chapel.

GREAT STUKELEY, CHURCH OF ST BARTHOLOMEW

This card of 1926 looks along the north aisle towards the east window, alongside which are several monuments to the Torkington family. The Torkingtons inherited the estate in 1565 through marriage into the Stukeley family and gave up The Hall as recently as 1901. At the time of the Parliamentary Enclosure the village was "rearranged" to create a park around "The Hall". The indent of a Stukeley Brass lies in the floor just this side of the rail.

GREAT STUKELEY, SCHOOL GROUP 1915

Today's children take holidays abroad in their stride, for these Church of England School pupils a trip to the seaside would have been quite an adventure!

WANSFORD, THE BRIDGE

Our third journey commences at the northern boundary of the county at the River Nene. The arch to the extreme right bears the date 1795, the adjacent three arches are from the 1670's these are in Sibson cum Stibbington and are in Huntingdonshire. The smaller ones beyond, constructed in 1577, lie in Wansford and are in the Soke of Peterborough. The river was spanned by a new bridge further to the east in 1929.

SIBSON CUM STIBBINGTON, FLOODS

Taken in August 1912, this card shows George Eassom and George Gilbert navigating just south of The Haycock. Alfred Chambers drives his horse and cart. Behind the pig and astride the dappled pony is Charles Dixon.

SIBSON CUM STIBBINGTON, FIRE

A time when excess water would have been useful. I believe this card shows the damping down of the fire at Stibbington cornmills in 1909. The sender (and probably the photographer) writes that he "was wet through to the skin" in attending the blaze.

SIBSON CUM STIBBINGTON, THE HAYCOCK STAFF

Gathered around a Daimler are some of the staff of The Haycock in the time of Captain White. The following names appear on the back of the card, Mark the Chauffeur, Letticia Wright, Mrs Coates, Alice Eassom, Ernest Gilbert and George Eassom.

Elton Hall

Markham's Oundle Series

ELTON HALL

Printed in Berlin, this card, one of the Markham's Oundle Series, shows the south east aspect of the Hall. To the right is the 15th century Gatehouse built by Sir Richard Sapcote. Adjoining the Gatehouse is an element added in the 19th century by the 1st Earl of Carysfort, using on the upper floor a bay window from the recently demolished Dryden's house at Chesterton. The centre block shows the remodelled 15th century Chapel. To the left can be seen the 17th century work of Sir Thomas Proby, modified in the 19th century. The tower is a 19th century addition. The property came into the ownership of Sir Thomas in 1617 and his descendants have occupied the Hall since that time.

Elton, near Peterborough.

ELTON, MIDDLE STREET

Published by Taylor and Downs of Peterborough and Stamford this card shows on the left the stone bays to No 5, a 17th century building, awarded an Historic Building Restoration plaque in 1986. Hidden from view is a pump. The Elton village store and post office lies behind the tree. Across the street the house has been replaced by Page's Cottage. The wall and gate have survived.

ELTON. THE GREEN.

ELTON, THE GREEN

Posted in 1910 the card shows No. 15 Duck Street to the left and beyond the Old Bakehouse, now without it's chimney. To the right in the distance is the former Girls School, the gift of Jane Proby. Behind the tree is the 17th century Crown Inn. These days the house to it's right has four windows in the wall facing The Green. The thatched 17th century building to the extreme right has gained a porch since this photograph was taken and there is now a corrugated iron roof to the adjacent barn. The Maypole no longer stands on The Green.

MORBORNE

Just over one mile east of Elton the Old Bullock Road runs south towards Alconbury. Our journey takes us from the A 605 down to the B 660, where we turn east for Glatton. On our way we shall pass to the west of Morborne Farm. This Jerome card was posted in 1936 and shows a rick raised upon stone stack rests.

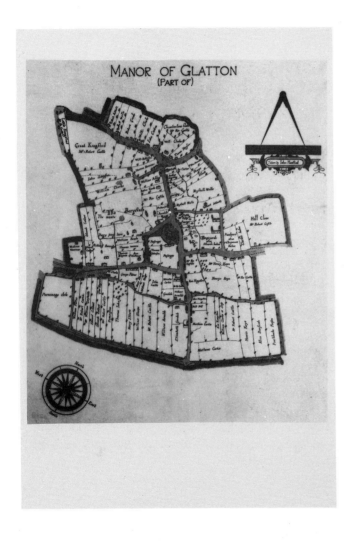

GLATTON, 1663 MAP

In 1663 John Hausted produced a map of the Manor of Glatton. This 1934 card reproduces the heart of the village. The compass and the dividers appear in the original manuscript. The map, which measures approximately 4 x 8 feet, is preserved in the County Record Office in Huntingdon.

GLATTON, SCHOOL

Release!! Since this scene was captured the porch and the schoolroom have been demolished. Posted in 1908 the sender seems to be either a Schoolmistress or the wife of the Schoolmaster, "this is a picture of our school and house".

GREAT GIDDING, GAINS LANE

As we enter Great Gidding from Glatton we take the first turn to the left and then turn right towards Chapel End. After approximately a quarter of a mile Gains Lane descends to the right. The house beyond the foot path climbing the bank has been replaced by a large Leylandi hedge behind which now stands the New Footpath House. The house just visible through the trees on the left is being restored.

LITTLE GIDDING

The church of St. John Evangelist at Little Gidding is pleasantly set on a hill side in the wolds. This superb Eagle Lectern dates from the late 15th century and was presented to the church by Nicholas Ferrar, the founder of the remarkable religious community. The community existed for approximately 25 years from 1626. The British Library possesses some of the Concordances produced at Little Gidding. Also shown in the photograph is the 17th century hourglass holder.

SAWTRY,
SIR WILLIAM MOYNE
AND WIFE MARY

This fine 1404 Brass Memorial was moved from the old into the new All Saints church in 1879. Sir William is in mail and plate armour, behind his head is the family crest. Mary wears a close fitted garment and an overmantle. Her elaborately dressed head rests on pillows. Sir William served in France under the Black Prince, represented Huntingdonshire in Parliament and was Sheriff of Huntingdonshire and Cambridgeshire.

CROSS KEYS, SAWTRY.

SAWTRY, CROSS KEYS

This card was published by Lane and Westerman of Sawtry and posted in 1928. Greenways shopping crescent has replaced the buildings on the left that once included the Cross Keys. Straight ahead to the left are now R. & J. Landrovers and to the right the offices of Cornerstone, the Abbey National estate agents.

VILLAGE GREEN SAWTRY.

SAWTRY, VILLAGE GREEN

This card was sent in 1911. To the left geese feed on the green behind the premises until recently used by Colletts the butchers. The thatched Chequers is now a private dwelling with the bay window carried up to the first floor. The barn no longer stands on the Green but the houses to the left are still much as shown.

SAWTRY, CHURCH STREET

Mr Slater the photographer was standing alongside No 7 Church Street. Further down the road the porch of the church hall is just visible. The thatched cottage standing end on has been removed and No 23 has been built to this side. Across on the right the cottages have also disappeared. Annesley Close is now immediately to the right and Park Road a little beyond.

SAWTRY, BRASS BAND

Posted in 1909 this card shows the band in the grounds of Conington Castle. The section of the building in view was erected in the early 17th century by Sir Robert Cotton. He collected many ancient documents dispersed from the monasteries at the dissolution and had used them to great effect in the service of James 1st, the son of Mary Queen of Scots. The arch, one of eleven, is said to have been acquired from Fotheringhay Castle, the place of Mary's execution. The Cotton manuscripts form an important collection in the British Library. The Heathcote family restored the Castle in the 19th century but the building has now been demolished.

SAWTRY, LAND GIRLS

With the young men of the village away serving on the front agricultural production was maintained with the help of the land girls.

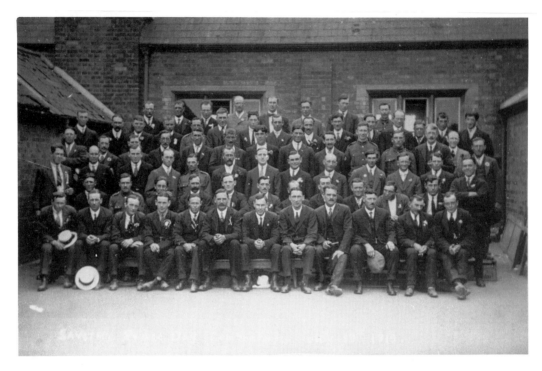

SAWTRY, 19TH JULY 1915

In the First World War the commitment of manpower to the Forces was massive. Here the survivors gather on 'Peace Day'.

SAWTRY,
EX SERVICEMEN'S HUT

This memorial board in the Ex Servicemen's Hut on the Gidding Road honours those who did not survive in the service of their country in the 1st World War.

SAWTRY, MR SLATER AND FAMILY

Percy Slater lived alongside the Green and was a well known photographer. Several of his cards are reproduced in this volume.

SAWTRY, YOUNG PEOPLE

A Slater photograph.   What brought these eight young people together?   What became of them?

SAWTRY, VE DAY

Alfresco tea in the Chequers Yard. How many of these children remained in the village?
How many found their futures to be elsewhere?

SAWTRY, VJ DAY
Another alfresco tea, this time alongside the Church Hall in Church Street.

Stilton, near Peterboro'.

STILTON, MAIN STREET

From the days when the York Road passed through Stilton but before white lines segregated the north bound traffic from the south bound. On the right is The Bell. The existing structure dates from 1642 but there was a predecessor in 1515. In the 1730's the landlord Cooper Thornhill supplied his customers, breaking their journey along the Great North Road, with cheese produced in the Melton Mowbray area. In time his merchandise became known as Stilton Cheese. Across the road were two further Inns, The Royal and The Angel, the latter dating from at least 1613.

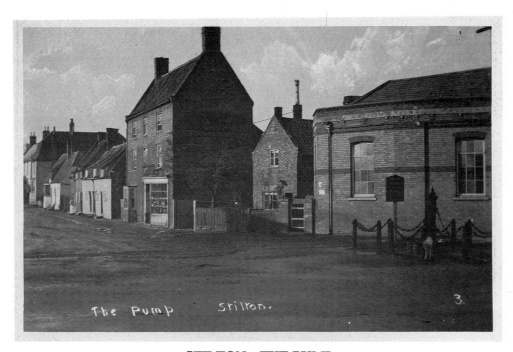

The Pump   Stilton.

3.

STILTON, THE PUMP

At the junction of Main and Church Streets the pump stands before the united Methodist church of 1864. The Stilton Stores now occupies the site (building?). Further along bow windows flank the recessed door of a shop. The large white characters which today spell out "E. Smith, Grocer, General Stores" do not appear to be present on this card posted in 1905.

Nene River, Water Newton

WATER NEWTON, RIVER NENE

Within the parish of Water Newton lies the Roman settlement of Durobrivae with it's extensive pottery manufactories. Now displayed in the British Museum are the important Roman early christian silver vessels and plaques found in 1975. This scene is far removed from those distant industrial days. The building beyond the fishermen has lost it's boathouse. The 1791 Watermill downstream was restored by Peter and Suzi Farrell in 1991 to provide attractive riverside apartments.

GENERAL VIEW, WATER NEWTON.

WATER NEWTON, THE OLD NORTH ROAD

In spite of the marching line of telegraph poles it is hard to believe that this really was the arterial route between London and the North. This section of the road is now cut off by the dual carriage way sweeping around to the right (to the west). The card was published by H. Saddington who ran the post office in the house to the right. On the opposite side of the road is the building known today as Neal's Cottage. The church of St. Remigius can be seen on the extreme left.

NORMAN X HOTEL.

NORMAN CROSS, HOTEL

Northmannescros was the meeting place of a Hundred and probably reflected the Danish presence. The hotel at the junction of the A.1 with the A.15 to Peterborough has been demolished but in it's place there now stands the new Forte Posthouse.

CONINGTON
QUEEN MARY'S CHAIR

All Saints church at Conington
was probably built by the Cotton
family in the mid 1500's. The
church is notable for it's fine
tower and for the Cotton
monuments. This chair once
stood in the chancel and is said to
have been the one from which
Mary arose to face her
executioner. The chair is
considered to be of late 14th
century date, much restored in
the mid 19th century.

CONINGTON, CASTLE FETE

A Slater photograph showing a game worthy of "Its a Knockout". The wheelbarrow pusher clearly runs the risk of a soaking.

HOLME, CHURCH STREET

Through traffic now passes around Holme leaving the village relatively tranquil and unobserved. In this picture we are standing alongside No 14 and looking towards the church of St. Giles. Since this photograph was taken both the thatched cottage and the chimney at the rear of No 16/18 have been demolished. The modern road is edged by kerb stones preventing the grass verges encroaching upon the carriage way.

Holme Station. G.N.R.

HOLME, RAILWAY STATION

With considerable engineering skills the Great Northern railway line was laid across the fen edge in the mid 1800's. At Holme a branch line ran across the fen to the Ramsey North terminal. This view looks down the main line towards Peterborough from the level crossing on the Holme to Ramsey road. The lower advertisement on the up platform (to the right), proclaims that "Keatings Powder kills bugs"! The station is no more. Overlooking the automatic barriers, the Holme signal box now stands this end of the former down line platform.

THE RAMSEY INCENSE-SHIP.
SILVER PARCEL-GILT, WITH RAMS' HEAD FINIALS. ENGLISH; LATE 14TH CENTURY.
L.11'3in. (GIVEN BY C. W. DYSON PERRINS, ESQ.)
M. 46. VICTORIA AND ALBERT MUSEUM. M. 269-1923.

WHITTLESEY MERE, INCENSE BOAT

In 1851 William Wells, the Lord of the manor of Glatton cum Holme, and colleagues, using the newly invented Appold centrifugal pump, set about draining the Mere. Joseph Coles, squelching through the mud, picked up an "ancient lamp". It was soon apparent that the lamp was a silver gilt Censer. Also found was this Incense Boat. Mr Wells gave the finders £25 for the objects which in 1905 changed hands for £1,100. The Censer and the Boat, both from the Abbey at Ramsey, were fashioned in the 14th century.

St. Mary's Village, near Ramsey

H. King, Ramsey, Hunts.

RAMSEY ST MARY'S

This card, published by H. King of Ramsey, was posted in 1903. To the right can be seen Eynesbury House, once a butcher's shop with it's own slaughter house. The little old boys used to be able to buy their sweets in another shop just opposite. Further along was the Red Cow and a harness maker who served the self-contained community that once existed out in the fen.

Church and Bridge, St. Mary's, Ramsey

RAMSEY ST. MARY'S

The church was constructed in 1858 to serve the settlers moving onto the recently reclaimed land. Whittlesey and the smaller Trundle and Ugg Meres were finally drained in 1851. The water course is that of the Old Nene River which once carried the water away from Whittlesey Mere. The brick arched bridge has been replaced with a ferro concrete construction. In 1922, seven years after this card was posted, the broached spire of this church endowed by Miss Emma Fellowes was removed. The weathercock, minus the bird, now rises above a square tower.

HARVESTING WITH BOAT. RAMSEY. AUGUST 1912.

RAMSEY, FLOODS

In spite of the efforts of the drainage engineers the water occasionally overcame the land with the result that in August 1912 it was, as the card says, necessary to use boats to bring in the harvest. This was the scene in the Bill area of Ramsey. In the background is Gull House once the home of Mr Pettitt the Molecatcher.

Catch Water, Old Fen, Ramsey, Hunts.

RAMSEY, HEIGHTS

At several places along the fen edge clay was extracted to make bricks. One such site was at Ramsey Heights. The locally produced yellow brick was used to build the houses in the new settlements. In 1854 John Summers combined brick making with selling beer and George Harris farmed and made bricks. It seems that Ramsey bricks were used as ballast on the ships transporting prisoners to Tasmania. On arrival the ballast was used to build the detention blocks. The brick pits and an adjoining building are now used as a nature centre.

Upwood House,   Upwood, Hunts.

UPWOOD HOUSE

The Lords of the Manor of Upwood have included Earl Ailwyn, one of the co-founders of Ramsey Abbey and members of the Cromwell family. The card, published by Freemans of Ramsey, shows the east front of the house built in the mid 1600's. From a century later we have the smiling ghost of Thomas Hussey who just before his death in London had rescinded his opposition to his daughter's suitor. Assured by the demeanour of her father's ghost Maria married Captain Bickerton who in 1778 became a baronet. Their son, Sir Richard, was second in command under Nelson.

RAMSEY MERESIDE, SCHOOL GROUP 1912

Photographed by Ketton of St Ives and Ramsey the card shows the school gathered apparently for a Christmas photograph.

Main Street, Farcet.

Copyright Fct. 2

Raphael Tuck & Sons Ltd. London

FARCET, MAIN STREET

This card by Raphael Tuck & Sons was posted in 1938. The methodist church in Farcet is notable for it's links with the west country Bible Christian sect. The Goldflake advertisement has gone but the shop remains, trading as T.C's Stores. The single storey building indicates a working farm that still retains access on to Main Street. The view is closed by the Infants School, now serving other purposes.

STANGROUND, BRONZE AGE BEAKER

In 1925 this fine beaker, seven inches in height, made some 2,000 years B.C. was discovered on the site of the Old Manor House in Stanground. The card was produced as No 12 of The Peterborough Museum Series.

ORTON LONGVILLE CHURCH.

ORTON LONGUEVILLE, CHURCH

Written on the back of the card is the following "Nice little church where all the Lord Huntleys are buried". Holy Trinity stands next to Orton Longueville Hall, once the home of the Gordon family, Marquesses of Huntley, Earls of Aboyne. The lamp no longer lights the entrance way and the large trees have been felled. The notice by the gate reads "The public are requested to respect and protect this churchyard. Any person taking flowers from this churchyard will be prosecuted. By order of the Rector and Churchwardens". The gates have been replaced since this photograph was taken.

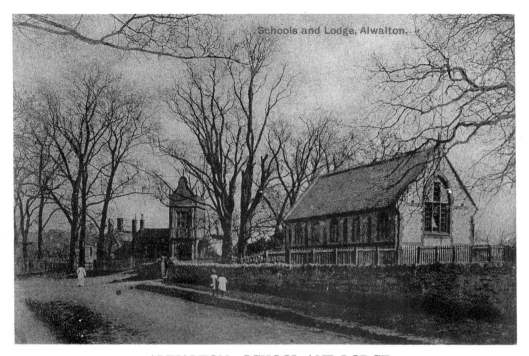

ALWALTON, SCHOOL AND LODGE

One of the T.W.R. Series this card was posted in 1906. In the distance is the Lodge. This is the rebuilt porch from Chesterton House, the home of the Dryden family until demolition in 1807. The porch dates from about 1625. The Lodge is in the care of the Landmark Trust. The school has been refurbished as offices, dormers have been introduced into the roof and the end window has been modified. A plaque at the entrance to the building records the fact that "Henry Royce, co-founder of Rolls Royce was born in Alwalton in 1863".

103

FRENCH PRISONERS MEMORIAL, NORMAN CROSS. 110.

NORMAN CROSS, FRENCH MEMORIAL

Erected in 1914 by the Entente Cordiale Society this bronze eagle commemorated the prisoners of war held between 1797 and 1816 in the large purpose built barracks at Norman Cross. Approximately ten thousand men were detained. They were mostly Frenchmen. One thousand seven hundred were buried in the adjacent cemetery. Craft objects made for sale by the prisoners can be seen in the Peterborough Museum and in the Norris Museum in St. Ives. The memorial was recently damaged beyond repair by vandals who stole the eagle.